Puss 'N Boötes

Dark Poems

Polly Alice McCann

Flying Ketchup Press
Kansas City, Missouri

Appreciative acknowledgments to the publications in which the following poems previously appeared: Blue City Poets in 2019: "July Blue." "Comeback Whales" which appeared in 365 Days Anthology in 2020.

Flying Ketchup Press
11608 N. Charlotte Street
Kansas City, MO 64115

Library of Congress Cataloging–Publication Data
McCann, Polly Alice.
Puss 'N Boötes: Dark Poems / Polly Alice McCann
Library of Congress Control Number: 2020908282
ISBN–13: 978–1–970151–14–5

To the Fire, the Cave, to the Earth and the Sky, to the tellers of tales, to weavers of starlight, and to Starlett and Diamond and Rosey, and to women authors of all stripes; to everyone who wore pink hats with cat ears and said #timesup.

To the Flowers who taught me how to talk and to the Stars who lead the way here and the Rose who gave me hope.

LETTER FROM THE AUTHOR

Dear Friends,

This book was inspired by two old tales that appeared in my poetry beginning two years ago. "Puss in Boots," a tale of a cat with feminine wiles rescuing a man from poverty and homelessness, and "Boötes" the constellation myth of a hunter. I spent two years looking to write poems that would somehow connect these two ideas. Finally, I centered on a favorite story, "The White Cat" written by Madame d'Aulnoy and first published in 1698, an epic novella of an enchanted woman hiding in an underground kingdom. She solves the dilemmas of a prince through having creative foresight and ingenuity to share her rare and valuable treasures with the world above. Some of these included yards of fabric that could fit through the eye of a needle, and the world's smallest dog (TouTou) that could fit into an acorn. Some of the imagery seems to have inspired the work of Frank Baum, Perrault, and other writers. The White Cat eventually becomes disenchanted and returns to the world above as a human once again.

As I centered on the theme "coming out from the dark," characters emerged: Red Riding Hood, Dorothy of Oz, Eve, and more constellation myths. These stories of empowerment and recovery re–imagine the feminine. They push the cultural expectations of hierarchy and power to a different set of values. To value relationship over control, creativity over usefulness; journey over results; acceptance over isolation; and the spirit of collaboration and intuition or "spirit" overall.

What these poems taught me: It's alright to approach dark emotions because through the process, we see how to find the light. Let's come out from our underground kingdoms where we've been hiding. Let's not bury imagination and creativity and delight. Instead, let's embrace the journey and learn from each voice.

Polly Alice

TABLE OF CONTENTS

LATELY POEMS ARE KNOCKING ON MY DOOR

They know I made a place for them.
I cleared out a room and decorated
it with a simple white bedspread.
Over the old doublewide, a few colorful
throw pillows. I hung up some old
folk art, the macramé owl
and put out a sign in the window
Poems, free lodging.
Then I let them in
fed them
potato soup
and homemade
gooseberry pie.
and let them tell
me their story.

"Curdie dared not stop to think. It was much too terrible to think about. He rushed to the fire, and thrust both of his hands right into the middle of the heap of flaming roses, and his arms halfway up to the elbows. And it did hurt! But he did not draw them back. He held the pain as if it were a thing that would kill him if he let it go — as indeed it would have done."

~George MacDonald,
The Princess and Curdie

FIRE

Tree Dream

When wood burns
in the fire, ghosts
rise up
in smoking branches
to tell you the dreams of what
they might have been.
How many times have I thanked
God for the fire where so much
was lost, where so much was
lost?

EVE LOOKS BACK

It used to be easy. I had everything.
My grandkids think Eden was when we
walked around with goosebumps, eating
berries and nuts—and had twigs in our hair.
Where do you get that? Sometimes,

I think it was all a dream,
but how would I explain eight hundred years
of nightmares and a century of bliss?
You would not have believed those trees.
They aren't like the ones here. My favorites—
the yellow pears— twice as large as those
bitter little things we call pears now. Ours
tasted like cinnamon. No core, only caramel inside,
the seeds were so small you could eat the whole thing.
I'd cut down the largest and cook fruit soup,
every Saturday.

Yes, we had fire. God, we weren't primitive.

It was too hot to wear clothes, and they
would have been a bother, because
we were always swimming
up waterfalls or going down
to talk to the fish and the merpeople.
They had such wonderful recipes for
hair cream—the merpeople I mean.

Don't even give me that look...

Anyway, I had the most magnificent hair.
Flowing all the way down to my ankles.
It was silvery blue, almost purple. God,
back then Adam had
only to run his fingers through my
hair and I felt like a double
rainbow. Little feathers would fly
right out of my head and float
on the breeze…kind of like dandelion
fluff you would call it.

That's how we had so many children.
No, we weren't like the animals back then.
Everything was always so... comfortable.
The wind would carry the seeds around
plant them somewhere in the garden and
we'd find them...babies popping up like weeds
in the cabbage bed. If they landed too far,
the storks would bring them back when
they were ripe. Adam had
trouble finding names for them all, we
had to start asking the monkey's to help us
come up with new ideas. Of course, there was
a big riot because the birds wanted to
help too. But we couldn't pronounce
what they came up with, let alone
spell it.

God, yes we could read and write. Who have
you been listening to?

Babies were so much easier back then.
They could walk a few hours after birth.
They loved to drink milkweed. They
played with the animals. We had several
nanny goats to heard them all until
they were full grown at the end
of each summer. The goats made fresh
cheese and butter for all of them—
taught them to talk, called them their kids...

Yes, animals could talk. Who has
been telling you animals never talked.
I heard them myself. Who do you think
taught me to talk?

If you can't believe your poor Granny
at her age, this conversation is over!

WOLF TALK ◆

The wolf came home wearing his usual
sheep's clothing and cardigan,
carrying plastic flowers and
wearing grandma's cap.
He stood under an Eden light
and with those glasses he was handsome,
but Red Riding Hood suspected he was the devil.

He sat down to dinner and immediately
complained her eyes were too weak
to see the eggshells she left in his omelet.

I have new glasses, the better to see you with, Wolf.

Your ears then are dimming, the wolf explained,
He hadn't said eggshells, he's clearly said
pepper because the dinner was too hot!

Last week, I had a wise chipmunk check my ears.
Red pulled the script from her pocket.
'said I have the hearing of a sixteen—year—old,
the better to hear you with,
the doc told me so.

After dinner, they cleared the dishes for
RRH to wash later. She tried
to tell about her day with the mice, and the
magic pumpkin growing in the yard.

The wolf pointed out, surely she had details
wrong. Her memory
was not what it should be.

Now you and I know RRH's memory
was shot through with holes.
I blame the wolf's teeth
biting her accidentally in the night.
Red fasted most days,
living on rice and cabbage,
sewing her own jacket and hood,

mending with threads that kept breaking.
In fact, RRH knew her head was barely attached
since that last time it had been knocked off.

But that's where her secret weapon lay.
You see, she'd been to town
to a specialist and she'd had her memory
tested by a wise old owl in a treehouse
on the Plaza. It cost a month's salary
in baskets of fresh bread.

She grabbed a folder of papers from
the hall table, green as grass in spring,
and waved the results a white flag–proud
as a banner.

Good news, I had the wise owl run tests.
I have 97% memory, the better to remember
who you really are, and
what kind of teeth you show.

She handed him the note from the doctor.
Out of a hundred women my age.
I'm in the top three for memory.
She put her hand on the Wolf's shoulder.
I'm not blind, or deaf, or dumb,
I'm just me. I'm just a girl who used to wear a red scarf
and I'm going to put it back on today.

The wolf said nothing. It was as if an ax
had fallen to his door–like he'd been tied
and gutted. Like he had rocks in his stomach.

He sort of disappeared after that.
No one knew what happened to him.
The neighbors said he's never kept up his yard.
Made RRH and the woodland creatures do all of it.

Except for her brother the woodsman and
grandmother, who showed up the next day,
I'm not sure anyone ever thought of him again.
They stayed together quite happily for some time,
and they may be there together still.

GAS LIGHT

The little blue bathroom
held an oil lamp with a wick
as wide as a girl's belt
You said sorry you broke it
and your mother said
—*These things happen*—
her mercy like feathers
over broken glass.

You went years without breaking
anything. You carefully fixed
the vacuum, the dresser,
the wall, bruised egos, your dress.
Sewed everything shut, even
your eyes so seems wouldn't show…

Still, through the seam the light dimmed.
—*The sky used to be blue*—you said.
You thought everyone pretended
not to hear, but you couldn't see
we were signaling you with our
upcast eyes reflecting the blue of the sky
off our very souls.

The trouble with a part–time gaslighter
—*there is no relief*—
you can never prove the lamp
existed, any more than it became dim.
Most likely, it's all your fault, for believing
that darkness isn't light and always has been.

 One day, you woke up and tried to say
—I used to be able to dance, drive a car, sing, even
solve for x in a problem as long as my arm—
but you'd forgotten how to speak aloud.
The light kept dimming. You couldn't see
the numbers on the phone, your shoes,
the gas pedal on the car.

So you took paper and pencil and solved for x,

then ripped the problem into bits. The papers, they stuck
to your head, your face. The numbers filed
down your arms into long white rows until
they made wings.

When you brushed them over your lashes
you could see again then you rose in the air
circled twice then flew away.

The trouble is, with a part–time
calculator, once you run away
you can never prove there
was any equation at all, except
you can see those wings
made of the number of times
you wanted to escape. Numbers
don't lie, they spell out freedom.

Enough of them in a small grate
make a nice fire better than any lamp.

Someone said–
–*These things happen*–
and you could only repeat
the alphabet
except you forgot the last letter
and ended with Y?

Easter Egg

Used to live in an Easter egg
the colors of the rainbow
yellow, pink and red.
Talked to the walls, yelled
stage set every afternoon
Don't remember my name if I ever
had one. Started to think.
Found a pencil and drew a little door
and a clock. She was a pretty one,
and when her hands said *three*, they reached
out, opened up the door. She said, *Run*!
Didn't know why my thin little legs were smarter
than my neck but they were the only part of me
that knew I was worth saving. Kept running,
Past a hat stand, a million acorns and
a liquor store along the highway,
where there is no room to walk.
Kept going toward the country
until a 1960 Ford picked me up named
Rosey. I came to a house with sheep,
a goat and a one–eyed dog.
The family said they'd take me in,
they said birds like me were
rare and wonderful.

WINTER WHALES

Whales are making a comeback,
they say. It's the darkest day of the
year, but sunny as an orange.
By the Christmas tree
with coffee in my mermaid mug
the lights are portals to the old
tree at Grandma Ray's, in the slap–
down house in St. Joe.

The roof parted to one side
sloping almost to the ground,
garland over the fireplace Alvin
built. Smooth red stones, round,
bright as friends. The
tiny porch a silent pause for the ice
gold doorknob,
always stuck but with a
push and kick, the thick carpet
relents, the door bursts
open its gentle maw to
a blast of heat and noise.

In the small paneled room
everything amber—
filled with song fire.
Sun-colored fruit hidden toeside
in stockings by the grate
and the feather foiled tree

flicker from the light of
dishes folding in and out of
the China cabinet
the dark presiding echo of the
coo coo clock cacophony
clashing with the Corningware clinks
and loud laughter chock full like
corn on the cob—

my you've grown so tall

Each one of these lights a door
each one of these lights a
match I want to strike.
It's been dark here for
so long.

Back in the quilted living room
I'm no longer small.
I'm looking for my
kites. What holds me here.
When I pull on the strings,

I see they aren't kites at all.
They are whales—I've tied
an epic ton of them
to each finger. I guess
reports are true, they have
come back
from extinction.

The Whales
fly me through a fiery sky
filled with colored stars
and I ask them *where we are going?*
They say that we never left
Grandma's house, and the
little dog, Lady, is still hiding
behind the couch next to the heat
register where the air blasts
out as hot as anything that can toast...

The warmth. The heat of that place
like being in the core of the earth.
—I meet a couple at Homer's Coffee.
They've been married for forty years.
The painting I bring them is about
sailing away to an island.

I just want a rest from double shifts both
second and third, working nights,
and weekends, sleeping through
dinner. I want to escape the cave.

We've been to an island off the coast
of Spain, they say
where you can cook your supper
outside—just dig a hole and use
the heat from the live
volcano. No fire needed.

Oh, let me sail to this island.
I'll bake you a potato, the kind
Grandma used to make. So hot
it could stay warm for hours.
Sometimes, I think that I'm still
running on the heat from
those moments.

When I was eight-years-old,
because I thought it was
hibernating, I let the box turtle
sleep in the garage all winter.
When I picked up that turtle
shell closed tight,
it was lighter than air.

That's the kind of light I don't need.
No, I want to wake up. I want to
come out clawing, ready to howl.
The turtles say I can come
back to life anytime
I want because

there are still pockets of
warmth in the old fire
from those hands
that held me and told me
I could come back
any time I liked.

Making a comeback.
The Whales say,
if they can do it,
I can too.

LIBRARIANS

Librarians are their own unique animal.
The women saunter in high heels or flats
like so many tigers the ink running

over their hides to camouflage
the fact that
librarians
are quick

burning a wick as fast as pages will carry
them— away from
their presence
away from their unstory
wrapped in so many sunrises
stamped with eyes that never close
at night

they chew on suspense
night hunters
—never looking at the dreary
stars in the jet blue sky
but only black letters
S's that wriggle like
snakes to become
story they hunt under
new moons as noir
as Nancy.

Librarians are their own unique animal
because after the soft ivory page turns
whispering in the night
they return to the library
and open its jaw, welcoming
the patrons to climb in,

sit around on its teeth
and celebrate the dark.
They light a fire and we dance
around it, holding hands

and finally understanding
the warmth.

How to Make a Poem Dive

First, make sure it's cold,
shivering, insecure.
Push him up as high as he will go
Tell him to win a Pushcart
To rattle and roll, to fly
to pound, and scream.

Then watch as he silently
mutters and climbs
back down unwilling
to make the plunge.

How to turn around a poem?
Tell him to take it out of first gear
Tell him to stop talking
about himself.
He'll say he has a grandiose
idea that you need to listen
to, but elbow him in the
gut to shut him up.

That's when he'll try second gear
He'll make it all about you
but not in a nice way.

When that doesn't work,
he'll get out his headphones
and pretend you're not even there
but just keep hitting him on the
back of his head with your pencil
until he's so annoyed, he's
ready to punch.

Grab him by the tail then
and introduce him to the
neighbors. Make him get out and stand
up on his own two feet.
Give him a task
like raking leaves
for the widow next door.

He'll want to slink back into the
swamp and sharpen his teeth.
Practice his tears. *You can't*
have that.

How to turn a poem around?
Wear him down. Take
him for a very long walk–
the desert is a good spot.
Wait 'til he's too tired to fight
you anymore. Until
he can't take one more
dry riverbed.

Then give him water
to drink and beer,
a cookout over the fire
with some friends, a soft
log to sit on. And as
the stars roll in
listen
to him sing.

"It would obviously take some getting
accustomed, I think, if it should be a
matter of talking into one's eyes that
which is up there outside the cave, in the
light of the sun."

~Plato, *The Cave*

BOÖTES

There are gaps here I can't account for.
Paper ones on the floor under the
kitchen table spilled out of the hole punch
stuck to the soles of my shoes–kids
are playing with guns for fun
shoot 'til you're the last one standing.
Why would this game work?
What about the game where
we add one then one more again.

I take my son outside to look
at the stars. So much ink
and so little paper. Like the words
in student essays from the college, inscribed
from the dust of Congo– Iraq– Ghetto,
so many wars hum on the radio as I drive
over the Buck O'Neal bridge–like so many
grackles on the roof of the flower shop
they flutter over Broadway
aimed under a tuffeted sky–
like punched out holes
as black as the dark between stars.

Dark, where I just want some light.
Sure, stars still shine on my back
porch and they have something to say.
Boötes broods there– a strange cowboy
with his dogs behind him–– he doesn't recognize
his mother because she has turned into a bear.

If there is one thing I want, it is
for my children to recognize me.
I want them to plow a new land
in whose gaps they plant little
seeds of expectation.

I am a mother bear who lost
her dark stripes, only the white
are now visible—like the whites
of my eyes hidden behind

Puss 'N Boötes

lids of pots and pans and supper plates
and the hairs under my chinny chin
chin aren't enough to hold me
here when the wolf has blown
away my dark words—my pages
empty of their ink.

Why did we never go out to see
the summer stars? Only Boötes
his walk with his hounds
our picnics always winter ones
in the deep plum colored cold.

But what if I took that sweet flesh back,
the dark back of my name,
the indifferent scars, those cold black skies
and poured them
into this bottle, would I have
enough ink to tell this story over?

If you break the heart of a poet
she'll write a poem about it.

If you mistreat a poet, a whole book
might need to be written

But if you steal the love of a poet
and crush it under your boots–
take the poets words and tear
the weft out of them, turn the poet
against herself until she ties
a gag over her mouth and forgets
her own name...

Then and only then you too
will be judged by the stars
not because poems were lost
or never written, but because
a poet was lost and so
too the stars.

When she returns, who will
be able to bear the words

she will have to say. There
will be constellations...

SHOOTS

Sleep in
to avoid facing a black day
brush my hair
it's another shooting
this time a synagogue

a people–
I haven't protested like water
signed petitions enough
to keep us from being this
place, this people

get up and grind beans
with mom
make bulletproof
coffee in the blender
with coconut oil

don't eat any food all day
put on shoes for a walk

listen to music
clean the kitchen
make rice for mom
bring in the hibiscus tree
Hibiscus for welcome, for
sweetness but it can't
weather a storm

put some greens to bubble
on the stove
paint the kitchen table
to match the new dishes

three generations of women
can't decide on a dish pattern
something to hold up
the world as it spins

why do we each think

a different color means joy
why does blue make one of
us sad and one of us happy?

start to paint a stencil
near the kitchen ceiling to lift us up
but mom says it's not good
maybe it should be hearts, I say
maybe it should be diamonds, she says

the paint dries green
as a copper penny
green as Lady Liberty
as frost on spring grass

I didn't walk into
full of yellow leaves falling
from the walnut tree like so much
confetti

drive down the highway
in my little red car
see a lane marked off with cones

never thought about leaves
settling on the road
never seen a road less traveled
never stopped to rest
because there is
too many roads
to search for
a place to belong

go out to meet people
never met them before
a writers group

know it's the writer's house
because there is a sign for a woman
running for senate out front
and a Buddha in the flower bed
smiling hands out.
why do writers love compassion so much?

why do they have to fight so hard to have the
freedom to love people to speak
to put the alphabet
together one letter a time?

why do they laugh in the dark and adopt
kittens escaped from violent ends?

why do they protect?
eat fresh bread together
and soup

what do writers
need?

a table they say
each other they answer
a rock to
rise out of the ashes from

and what if we all wrote
a new
story
together

what if...

Night Blooming Flower ❁

A late night knock on our door.
It was back in that little town near the
Susquehanna? That one where beautiful
poppies grew in front of white porches
where wreaths change on doors by season
and the old water mill still stands by the creek.

It's time.

I gather up the baby, put her on my hip.
No shoes. Quickly, we wander over
the stepping stone yard past crocus
and the mud smell of the nearby pond
The sky—orange and purple mixed
together.

Sue and Bob meet us at the mailbox
under their budding maple
heavy with seeds, across one lumpy lawn
through the dwelling dark. With hushed

murmurs, we step over roots and leaves
cracks in the sidewalk our expectant joy like
a river growing from winter runoff.
We enter the small white sun porch, cerulean
in the darkening night. The old screen door

slams and scuttles as we each bump
inside–one, two, three, four, five
of us join the others jammed around the wicker
chairs and table though none of us sit.

We mesh together legs and arms, neighbors
in sweaters and house slippers holding on
to each other–fingers lightly on shoulders
and hips so we don't crush
into the wonder.

There in the center

a shrub in a heavy ceramic pot
its trunk the size of a broom handle, leaves like
hands dark as ripe olives
sleek as magnolia leaves, and the proud mother
beside. Her smooth white hair like the buds
on the slowly opening flowers awakening
to the moonlight. Our bated breath like
small stars of warmth—we watch as the

blooms unfurl strong as teacups, open to the rising
moon their crepe paper petals so sure of themselves.

It only blooms once
in a lifetime and only
at night during a full moon.

Oh, to be a night—blooming flower to know that
for once in my long life, I would be beautiful,
I would be loved, and I would not
be afraid of the dark.

If I could go back in time, I'd take those flowers
to the cobbler and ask him to make a pair of shoes.
I'd put them on the baby
and teach her to walk like a woman who knows

her worth— knows that the world is not made
of poppies but of light that we could reflect
from the small of our backs and the
force of a firm mind.

SPADE ♠

Changing a fractal seems
impossible because in order
to make one change you will
have to alter it an infinite
number of times.

If your shape is, say a heart, with a small
break inside and in that shape is another heart
exactly the same shape with another small
crooked line.

You're right, it's impossible to
change the fractal because you are you
every day, and your heart beats the same way
most of the time. In other dimensions
you are yourself, just a different version of you
with the crooked smile and the same eyes.

So the equation equals the force of resistance
times a million versions of yourself
refusing to change.

The gestation of a poem is an interior
fractal that keeps building. It grows
in shape and multiplies itself a
zillion times—you must get the poem out before
it kills you, the small curve of its stem
breaking you into a million crooked
smiles.

Yes, you are doing this alone, raising
kids, cooking meals they don't like,
buying groceries in a hurry without a cart,
putting things back because you don't
have enough, but if you do this every
day every day and you stop to alter
one word, if you actually let
words leave your finger and turn
flip your heart upside down into a spade
you could dig your way out..

THE WHITE CAT

It's dark in here.
There on the ground,
I see a nine patch of suggestions—
some things are buried there.

La, they've been abandoned.
By who, is the question
I ask myself every night
when I fall asleep. Sleep is hard
to come by because the nightmares come
so often I can't fail to write them

down in a dream journal. Je journee
through each, and every day.
Nuit is when J'ai lis mes rêves,
Je n'ai jamais peur parce que
Je viens dans ce petit jardin.
I know what's buried here.
My lost hopes.

Amusante, how something can become lost.
Unlike a bundle of lavender or a braid of onions,
there is no scent to guide you; funny how you can
have a dream about things buried in the ground,
but you can't stand up to

tell them who you really are
because you've come from the dark—
a place where you were buried.

Resurrection is something these buried talents
dream about. Are they even still—
Alive is what you may be
when you share what's buried here.

BATTLE DRESS

There's a snag somewhere. We're   sewing the dresses, the dresses we
used to wear. The ones we made ourselves out of scraps and cast–offs…a
prom dress, a wedding one, and the pink one from that party. The one we
made ourselves. But now, the dresses, they are one–sided like this
constellation–this conversation with some light that is eons out of date and
our words are as they've always been, just us talking to the jays
on the breeze wind. When we look
back, we can't find anything
we really suffered. Not really any
bruises. We don't remember threats
but if we place on one side of a simple scale,
love, and on the other, indifference…which is
heavier? Well we can tell you. Indifference weighs
nothing at all, of course. And that is where the darkness
waits. For what is a star without mass? What anchors it in
place? Love. The weight might be equal to a whole ocean or
any number of stars in Orion's belt. There he is now. We see the
hunter leaving for the summer. He only lives in the sharp winter
indigo sky. And so maybe what we lost…was loss. What we lost, if
anything, is an infinite lightness of being–the weight of a firefly. What
we want to keep–the promise of summer, the strength of a trumpeting
orange blossom as fiery as a sun, the muscle of a Monarch ever orbiting,
the weft of satin grandma brought back from Japan after the war. And,
we do get to keep the dogs. Have you noticed when a dog sits in your lap
just how heavy they are…like they are from another gravity? That is love.
This basket of notions with grandma's thimble. Who's to say how far it will
go? At the right speed this small metal cap could stop a starship. You have only
this sewing needle for a sword but with it we'll sew up the holes and mend the
tears. Our tears will fall through bottomless buttonholes and arrive on a far–off
moon to create an ocean heavy enough to hold water people will need someday.
Here, now, with this thread, we can only take the old material so far until it's run
out. So, we'll dive into the night sky, reach for new constellations till we've woven
a fabric from starlight and sand– enough for shoes, capes, dresses–even a crown.
Enveloped in this new thing, we will no longer remember, no longer remember.

GERDA & THE SNOW QUEEN

You know the story where the boy
gets a piece of glass in his
eye from a dark mirror
that's ever after shattered.
Kidnapped by someone colder than
pure ice. He leaves his
family, lost to them?

 I used to think the girl
in the story was a hero—

taking the journey barefoot
to save her best friend.
She battles cold, hunger,
starvation, thieves, witches
until she finds the boy.
Nothing will save him

till a single
tear melts his heart
washing out the evil
shard— so he can see again. I used
to think she was a hero

but it happens every day. Every day
another one is given a dark glass.
I'm Gerda. What the storyteller forgot?
When someone you love
can't see you anymore because
everything is distorted, cracked,
you begin to believe the cascade.
You think the black ice knows

the real you. What the story doesn't tell you
is that you are not sure what to believe
anymore. What the story doesn't tell
you is how hard it is to remember
or believe life before the looking
glass slit all hope— before monsters
were the only trope.

Yes, Gerda took years to find her
friend scaling the northern world.
Who was there to rescue and help her?
Enemies. Even enemies helped
her—witches and thieves, her anger, a bear,
the small memory that once there was
something good worth saving
something called a rose and she
grabbed each thorn on the way up.

When you have lost your best friend
and there is no one to tell. When you traveled
for years and you find him
only to have him lost again. You feel like
the mirror has won and no love
can unbreak your heart no tears
will save you now

Cold. You're so cold.
Your feet won't walk further, your
boots are lost, your sled stopped high
in the mountains. In this version—
you may not be the rescuer, you
may not be the mountain climber,
you may not outwit the traps
to root you in place and make
your feet forget how to dance.

But when you get there into
that cave. Love anyway.
When you get there into
that cave. Love anyway.

MOTHER BEAR ✳ CASTILLO

On becoming a star
forty–two light years
space over time from
my home.
I saw over my shoulder,
a cave. I didn't mean to slip
I didn't even know I fell
so softly was the glassy
slope.

Panic, when I realized too
late what misfortune had
fallen to me, I peered up
to find the pitch, but I was
past hope. I felt my way back
night by night, pressing the
black universe with my
fingers to the find the

minute my life went dark.
But there were too many moments
not one. Hiding under the tablecloth
behind the den, hiding behind words
among night forests, surely my
life has always been swung
though a dark gate.

Louging home in shadows
after all the lamps were lit
finding fireflies because I could
see their beating wings even
in the darkening dusk.

I didn't know how dark
a lie could be then— so dark
that those same tales could
become extinguished.

I couldn't make a way out or
back so I recalled each

memory of the sun and the
moon and the stars, my family
the dogs, and birds.

Once I had sewn pictures
of them, I stitched my portrait
into the night, the fireflies
came and lit up
my work. There by the light
of my crown and staff,
my prayer of knots,
I could just make out the
way. Kneeling,
I felt for the
hardened imprint
of my former path
fell for the forgiveness
of my former steps.

I began to believe my old
life hadn't been a dream.
I spoke to each memory
aloud and to the moon I added
that she was handsome.
To the birds, I sang.
And to the sun
I asked for a rescue.

The dogs woke first.
I tied my belt to them and told
them to run home and they
carried me here. No one
will believe that I have been
a star, or conceive that it
meant I was in darkness.

I'm not sure the people here
even remember me. So I have
started again. I am still a hunter.
Still a shepherd. Still a protector.
I am a mother bear of all bears.
But I sleep now with the light on,
and I tell my dreams to stay bright.

"One word, Ma'am," he said, coming
back from the fire....Suppose we have
only dreamed, or made up, all those
things—trees and grass and sun and
moon and stars and Aslan himself.
Suppose we have. Then all I can say is
that, in that case, the made—up things
seem a good deal more important than
the real ones. Suppose this black pit of a
kingdom of yours is the only world.
Well, it strikes me as a pretty poor one.
And that's a funny thing, when you come
to think of it. We're just babies making
up a game, if you're right. But four
babies playing a game can make a play—
world which licks your real world
hollow."

~C.S. Lewis *The Silver Chair*

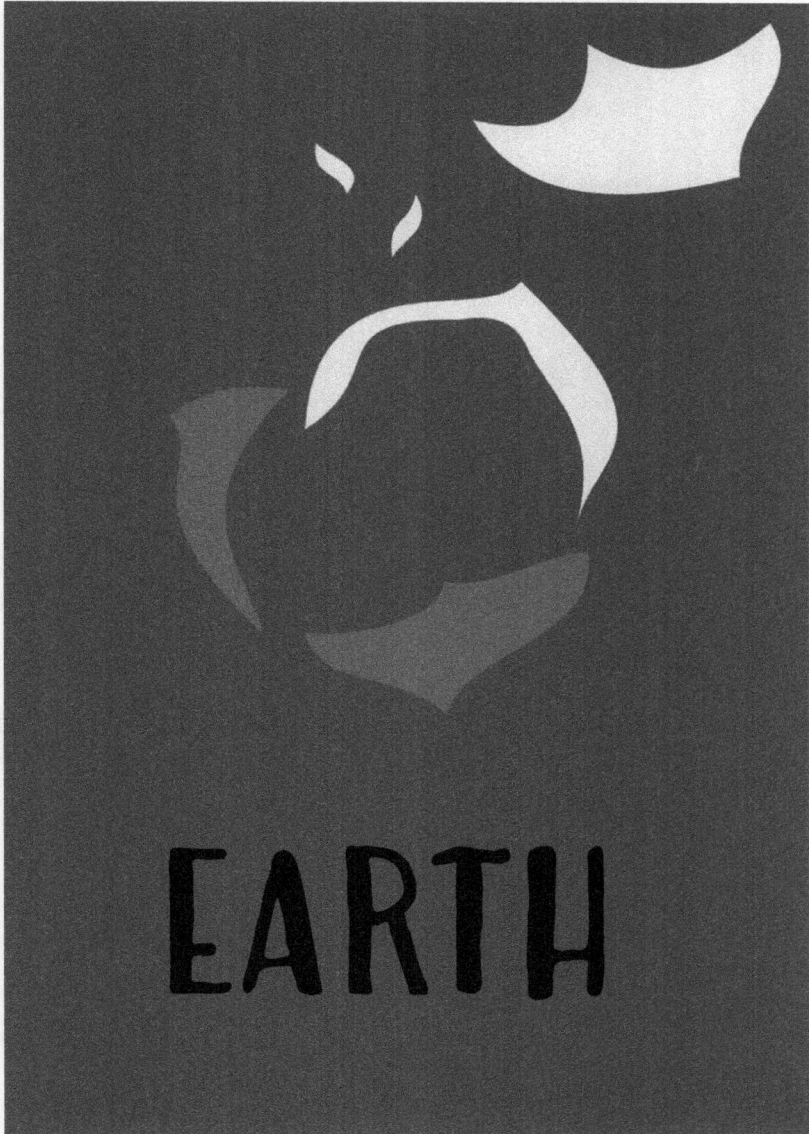

EARTH

How Many Times a Robin

How many times does a robin
dive his beak into the dirt
in faith a worm is there?
Does he trust the rain's
convincing drip to drive them,
or does he trust the worm
to do his job and breathe?

VINE

I bind this vine

a circle then a line

a line, a circle

ivy for friendship

marigold for sight

morning glory

reunion,

this wreath

re–mind me

everything and nothing

true vine

unending

light to half–light

unbroken

Forever,

PUSS 'N BOOTS

So, you think you've lost
everything but you're wrong—
here I am. Just look at me!
I'm the cat you've overlooked
from the start. The one who
stayed by your side
when Ol 'Man
didn't think you were smart enough.

So what if you don't
have a great education, I never
got any school.
So you don't have well… anything,
a farthing to your name.
Look at me, I'm not allowed
to own anything.

So your rat of a brother kicked
you out of your Dad's old place.
So you've got only the shift on your back.
So you haven't had breakfast.
Look at me, I'm skin and
bones. I get scraps to eat.
Look at my paws, I'm barefoot.
You. You. have boots
And boots make the man.

Well, aren't ya a man, or are ya?
Look at me, the only thing you own.
I can't leave but you
can go anywhere,
do anything, talk to anyone.

God, If I were a man, I'd
make it work. I'd have
a new job, a new name,
and a wardrobe to match.
I'd have people offering
me everything …

Give me your boots. That's
right. Take 'em off.
Give me your boots.
I'll fix everything.
Just promise me.

Promise me,
you won't forget
who saved your skin.

Downward Barking Dog Star

The dog has pulled me face down
in the mud and grass. I'm okay,
and now he seems kind of sorry.
I want to tell him that just because
some man with white hair and a cap
beat him long ago, before he was rescued,
—that not all white–haired men are bad,
and just because some boy on a bicycle threw
rocks at him once, not all people on bicycles
are bad. But somehow he is certain
everyone in a hat or with white hair
or with a bicycle must be his enemy.
I have no idea how to change his mind.
I mean whenever I see… a certain type
I want to bare my teeth and go for the jugular
So I tell myself that not all people are bad
just because one was.
Not all people with a certain eye color are
bad just because two eyes once were.
Not all people with chins are bad, just
because someone with a serious chin
had a lot of cheek—
Not all people of a certain religion are bad
just because someone who claimed
to have one, didn't—
You see the pattern, and no matter
how many Venn diagrams I draw,
I will still be lying face down
in the mud with my dog,
barking at strangers
until we mend, The only problem,
dogs don't understand Venn diagrams
and I'm not so great at yoga.

Broken Ring (Borealis)

I wanted to change something
but what would fix me?
//turn me inside
out and make me new?

I took off my old name,
put on a new one with satin trim.
//my old name –

I stomped it into little pieces
swore at it a little
//tore it up
hid it in the night.

I left it there
to shrivel up
get rained on–

//dogs walked over it
grass grew around it
flowers covered it.

I pretended it didn't exist.

When it was humble
//left for dead
I picked it up, dusted it off
then I wore it like a crown.

PENELOPE'S COFFEE ODYSSEY

When you go to the coffee shop
and you decide that you want to experience
something as strong as love and
as bitter as life. You take that first sip expecting
black earth, sweet fire, breathable air, holy water
but what you find is that this is not
real coffee. It is something that is about
the idea of coffee, but it's not coffee. And

that is when you know you have become someone
who cannot be happy unless your coffee is brewed
over a fire in a golden dallah then poured into a
thimble–sized porcelain. Communion thick
as the blood between brothers served by someone
like an Elijah who takes you to find a still small voice
You ride high, floating through the wasteland,
except your camel is at the end of the pack,
the bottom of a hierarchy only camels know.

The sky above you like an endless tablecloth
enough air no one could ever go hungry–
the valleys beside white paper cliffs
with enough space to write all those
words begging to be lined up, ordered, put into long lines
running east. So it feels natural sleeping out
under starless blind night, waiting for a pink dawn
that never comes. Half–frozen you lay your cheek on the
desert's cruel chest– and from its heart you write your
first poem that poem will be to fall in love with

a mirage, weaving on an endless loom of knots that
keep you wandering in circles until the
day you discover a diary he left. Not that it said
anything bad about you, not that it is full of
all the hidden secrets he kept. No.
It's only that you aren't in it. Since you
didn't make it into his book, since you
have never been loved, you decide
it's time to really live And you will
live as strongly and as bitter as a Bedouin

and as high as those cliffs you still feel around you
as fierce as that desert cold in your veins
and as faithful as that camel who knows where
water comes from—who knows where water comes
from, and who knows that at the end of the line
you can turn around and see the whole world
in front of you.

UNEDITED PRAYER GARDEN

Our gardener who art in heaven
succulents sprout anew like
hens and chicks plump like the little
plaster angel holding a puppy
Hallowed is thy name
among the carnations
shells and corals
tulips and pink daffodil
thy kingdom come
thy will be done among
the snails and roly–polies
among the robins planning
up for spring
the paving stones that say
there's no place like home
on earth in earth and
around the mums
as it is in heavenly holy basil
give us this day our strawberries
and pansies as heavenly blue
as cherubs' wings like all that
is good and holy let peonies
bloom like clouds
with silver linings and forgive
the little ants and woodlice
forgive the bees, the spiders,
the pealing paper birch tree
forgive the dandelions who are
only stars
forgive us, lord,
with moss and rain, and
lead us not– lead us not back
to winter
deliver us from drought and scorch
from powers from root rot. For
yours is this garden and
yours is the garden—and yours
is the garden. amen

Puss 'N Boötes

"Why do you stand there looking up
into the sky?"

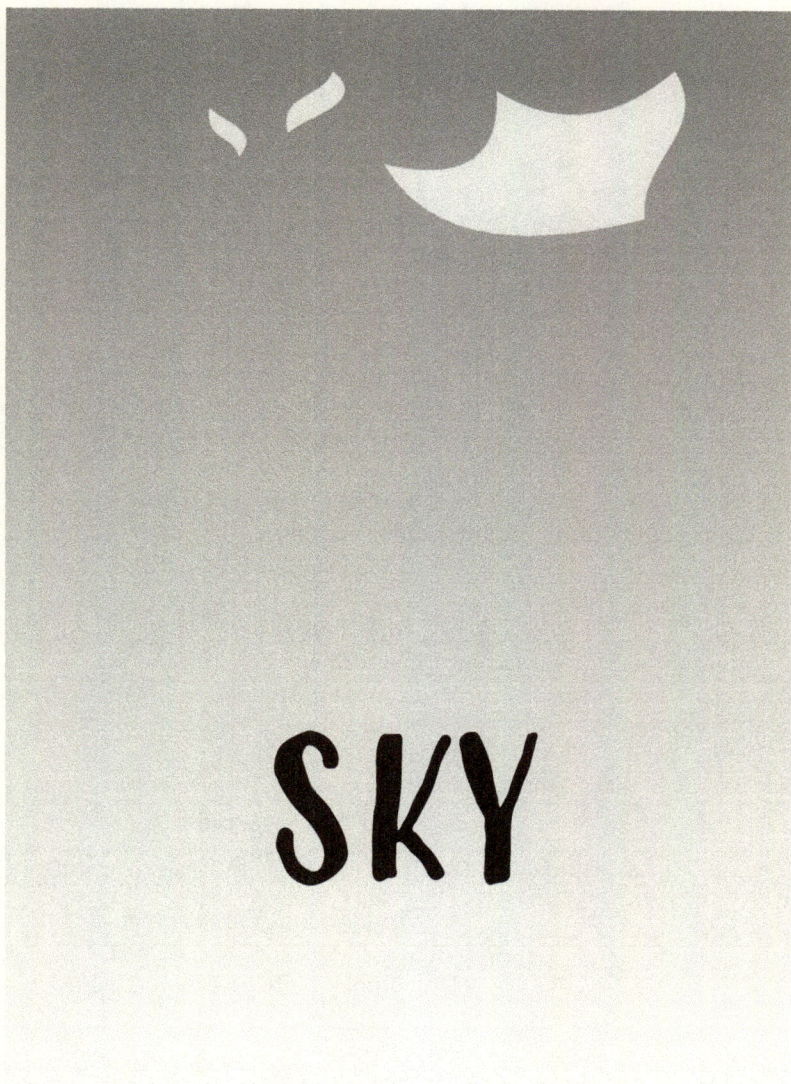

SKY

SWIFT⤵

On days I take a walk,
I must hurry back
to write a poem.

On days I write a poem,
I do not always take
a walk.

On days I walk, I pray.

This year I forgot to pray
or maybe I never stopped
praying– it's hard to tell
sometimes if I'm in renewal

or retreat. The world
is an owl pellet
of old bones on the path.

I am a grey mouse
in a warehouse.
I leave the studio late
in the evening. I'm
so stiff
I can barely
stand. My fingers still
covered in paint.

The gathering dark is quiet
ink. The sky, cyan– and one
chimney swift flutters and chats

his voice like
pages thumbed
in a book
he hovers around the street
light yet unlit
a dark strike in the
coming night.

I tie a string to the swift
and watch him circle–
the threads wrap around
my pinkie and I float
up into the yellow
of the dusklight
by a finger.

I'm Thumbelina
flying over the city
a world too big for me
hoping that when I
land someone
will stop and
take me to
a safe table, serve
me sweet tea and
tell me

the world is
your rose and
all the words
in your story
will be good
ones.

I'll tell you
a poem is
something we
love but don't–
love it too much–
for it must go on its way
again.

WHAT IF

So
what if
people   in their
natural   state were
more like
birds
if
we breathed easy, hummed over the stove, sang over folding
the tea towels pressing the seams to match. What if we
are more like birds than we first
believed

if we
could
just let go
we might sing.

SEQUINS

Mom and I drive to the Folly Theater
with the top down—the sky
our road—to get free
tickets to the baseball game.
Then to the stable
where S has been lunging a horse
in the shiplap white barn.

Dinner is leftovers from the
dinner party last night.
Five of us were together
eating Indian food around the table
reading a hybrid play
a spoken word poetical story.
Everyone smiles though it's
about someone who's just
about to find their truth.

I wonder why people love to
play parts, read lines,
to be someone else.
I wonder at friends around the table.
That such a time exists like this
when dogwood flowers rise,

ice tea gets watered down into
an evening of star talk.
Yeah, I know there are wars
going on and I'm the biggest
doubter in the Universe

but Poetry is my thankful cup—
where I put thread and buttons,
pins, and notions, sequins, the tiny
shiny things. I know the items of a day
listed out can never show the heart

the ragged edges the torn
parts mended. The seams
pulling, but here underneath I think

hope will spring up
and with those loose threads
I will sew on new wings.

W.W.D.D.

So I've always wanted—not the shoes—
from the Wicked Witch of the East
Silver or red makes no difference
they look uncomfortable
No. But I would like the tights.

Striped tights would
mean I was magical
that I wake up after dark
that I could project myself into
visions, write in the sky with smoke.

But usually, I don't think about that
I think about Dorothy.
What would Dorothy do?

She makes a plan, starts on a path
—really any path that might be
right without too much—
I can generously call it—
fact. And then she invites.

She invites someone
to come along beside her. Doesn't matter
what kind of person. Animal,
Vegetable, Mineral. She loves
them all. Their fears, she feels them.
Their wants, she wants them.
Why?

Maybe when you grow up in a flat
grey world without a friend
then you find a place where everyone
wants to tell you their story

and for the first time, people are listening
and for the first time, people are waiting
for you to answer and you know
you know you don't have all the answers,
so you simply say...*Come with.*

JULY BLUE 1986

The sky burns midnight
until the clouds burn
a lightning white calliope
I'm blinded by blue.

What do I remember?
My feet following Aspen steps
slung by the roots of trees.

Cicadas thrumming
until my bones resonate with their song,
paper fields of corn answer over my head
parched grey earth jips under my feet
soft like the smooth stones from a riveting stream
as dark as barn swallows.

The crickets beat the hot rhythm for my brain,
crrick–aaa, crrick–aaa.
My blood flows from top to tip in tune.
The cicadas treble a clock maker's cry;
winging the secret wheel of the world,
they trill a tambourine
trrranga, rrranga, thrrraaanngaaaaaaaaaa

Then silence
and again
trrranga, rrranga, thrrraaanngaaaaaaaaaa

Wave after wave calls louder in intensity
until they unzip the sun from the sky itself
cut out each triangle,
and roll it back into a paper collage of sound.

Unearthly soldiers, at their command
the trees dance.
The leaves shudder
flinging gold back into the sun
answering their call.
It rolls from the ringing globe
edges the clover and

slides across my back

until I am July Blue
and July gold
I am green with life
I am fire at night
I am hope at dawn's dark dew
I am the sound of a thousand stars singing
I am baked into a hard brown clay
steeled under a rainbow of white air
my song like skippers

Scissors

It's not a sewing circle, it's not crafts
it's not a lady's brigade or a bizarre
There's no Tupperware, not Avon but
here we are in January
under the blowing heater
in the sunny warehouse
west of Midtown. Cold as
white cotton, we sew and mend
around the makers' table at the
eco upcycling store. One embroidery
says *Fuck Cancer* another has no
words at all but we are safe
here in this space together with a bit
of string and sharing the scissors
between us.

LEMON MOON ◖

Coming over the bridge on a snowy evening
Birch trees lace
tapering tallest in the center
six unbroken arrows.
We are together.
We are one.
Coming over the bridge
on a snowy evening
the white trees lace
under a lemon moon
in the freshwater sky
Here in the lavender twilight
she may bathe and bloom
into an amaryllis
Dear one,
we will survive—

A double blossom
future awaits.

EASTER 2019

Easter comes in the morning
with eggs died in silk from India
with chocolates in fresh baskets
because mice ate the old ones

Warehouse 13 reruns on Amazon
are familiar after studio nights of
epic wonder in the warehouse
on thirteenth among the pots and pans
mannequins and dust bunnies.

So hard to understand
in a gluten–free world
how to be a sweet daily kind of person
as we sit and wait for the Muller report.

Good Friday is another art show
another day smothered in coffee
the walls sing– a show about women's
take on the world, and art may
be one of the only places left to speak.

Back at the warehouse, it's quiet
except for one sister adventurer.
They say God places the lonely
in families, and I am grateful.

Saturday is shopping for candy with
Alyssa and planting pansies in the flower
box. The gardener loads my little
red car with mulch and compost.

Sure, it stinks. But feed it, water it, it will grow.
Just how I want my heart to be

Reborn. Renewed like the endless supply
of milk and honey delivered
every Wednesday from Shatto dairy.
My pantry is full, my heart is fragile—

so I bake bread with
poppy seeds and wonder if the lilies
and roses I placed on the table are too
joyful for a time when some of us
are lost and broken, missing.

Sure hope seems small
but a white–throated sparrow came
to visit us this year.

He sings three long low notes
in his gruff little waiver, like a boy
practicing for the choir. Somewhere
is a bird in love.

And as long as the birds still believe
—I will remember
their maker and the one who said
he will rise with healing in his wings.

MACARONI

After the poetry festival
everything I say is a poem
all my words rocked in another person's rhythm
sweet like when we danced on the porch
or pushed off on the porch swing
our feet swooping up slowly
moving forward like
a canoe slipped to shore.
swinging back in time
back in time– back
when I could see the whites of people's
eyes and the pupil too
the iris, so blue, so brown, so green
green like the grass I rolled in as a child
covering me with tiny paper cuts
like my lips now
so cut with words
brown like the earth
grandpa grew strawberries in
so deep with roots,
blue like gathering ponds
on every nearby farm,
refracting, reflecting light like lips
bruised blue from a hundred words
knocked sideways by elbows of songs
remember that song we used to play on the piano
that guy who went to town stuck a feather in his
hat and called it something?
That's how I feel after three
days and three nights of words
words that I'll never get tired of
words that mend my broken harp
one string at a time. If I had a name
for it, I'd call it something too,
and if I had a name for it...

"I daresay you'll see her soon," said the Rose. "She's
one of the thorny kind."

"Where does she wear the thorns?" Alice asked
with some curiosity.

"Why all round her head, of course," the Rose
replied. "I was wondering you hadn't got some
too. I thought it was the regular rule."

~ Lewis Carroll

ROSE

GRACE

Grace is not the gentle drip
after a summer rain,
but a gasp of breath
from the nearly
drowned.
Grace brought us
to the place we dreamt
by desolation, not by destiny
by drowning, not by boat.

St. Valentine's Day ♥

One day I wake up
to no school.
Just mom and me.
She pulls out paper as long
as her arm—reds and pinks
and paper lace.

*Let's make valentines for
Dad,* she says.

But we haven't any glue.

We will make some!

Flour and water
make a paste applied with
a brush. Something from nothing.

There in the dining room
the silver and black Damask wallpaper
a forest, the table cleared, the sugar bowl
moved from its throne
the dark curtains open, we
work all afternoon.

She shows me how to fold
the paper, to cut
out a half circle to a single star's point.
Smoothed out, unfolded wings,
it becomes a heart. The magic of love
unfurled. I cut until my hands are tired.
My hearts small and jagged.
Hers with broad arms like
hugs. The valentines collected
and pasted on paper as tall as me.

Love, I decide, is larger than
my whole life. My dad's
face when he sees it. His eyebrows

raise in surprise. His mouth
a small "o" his cheeks as
red as construction paper.

I never thought about this
moment much before
until today. But I am sure
this is the day I found my secret love
for hearts, for paper, for things
that open. Something from nothing.

Today is Valentine's day
I go to Steel's Used Book Store.
Books with golden pages, their
aged threads, the glue
that binds them together
opening into hundreds of wings.

Then I write myself
a poem and listen
to the grateful dead
a poem about bitterness
a poem about life
and that's how I spend
Valentine's day
just me and a touch
of grey with
St. Stephen.

PRAYER KNOTS

Bodhicitta is a prayer
about compassion.

First, make a picture
of ashes because prayer is when
you come to the end
but you have
just enough spark left
for half a beginning.

Second, make a picture of
a knot. One knot. Because
after you come to the end of
yourself and you try to pray
you won't really begin praying
until you think of one other
person. Just one other
person that you can care about.
Throw your lasso and tie a knot
around their name.

Third, make two or three knots.
Because if you can pray for one
person you may think of another
person or another group you
want to pray for, a house, a town,
a city, or a planet, a tree, a forest or
a river– you will think of something
you wish was better, happier, more
peaceful and you will say,
Surely they deserve better.
Surely they deserve health,
wholeness, happiness,
family, love, restoration
*fairness...*so tie a knot for them.

Last, make a picture
of a smooth road
or a long ladder because
prayer goes both ways

someone has been pulling
you the entire time
helping your coming and going.
You are not alone.

You will see your enemy
is just someone's child.
Your friend has found
a family. The artist
has found someone
to hear their story.

The sick person
is made well. And most
of all, you have been
rescued.

And when you stand up again.
You are not ashes. You
are a small light–

and now the path is open
for you to walk again.

GATHERING LINES

It's artists' night and we gather around
perched on folding chairs
settling down in the old
couch that's just for decoration
and the wooden break room chairs
stable as boulders
Like birds colored every feather
we share and brag, question and
query. What is an artist
and if you call her a Rose
will she answer?

No name at the top
of the fifth–grade paper with
run–on sentences that
make my eyes water–
the sentence is like a car,
I tell him. *It's a little rolling vehicle*
and the verb is the engine
that makes it go.
The subject rides inside
sometimes with a friend,
but you cannot pack too
much into that car,
or it will not go.
My son laughs.

I cannot go with this,
I told the poet
whose words are like
a waterfall and a softly
bubbling stream like a
thunderstorm and like
rainbows–*the end of the line*
of a poem is important because
that end word stands out.
Poems need to be on
purpose, I say. *Everything*
about them must be intentional.

Intentionally, I cut out words
with black lines over
the text my high school
intern has written for three
months– his breath catches
in his chest as I say without
any platitudes or warning
to make the news easier to bear,
the essay is
stronger with fewer words.
Keep it simple

It was simple to bake the cookies
with the last bit of almond flour
where I did not follow
the recipe. When the artists
ask for it,
I'm not able to share
exactly what I did.

Sometimes–well all the time
I break my own rules. I use
too many words and I don't
care about the end of the line
I add honey but I don't call
it anything to squeeze out sweetness
from a honey bear's little yellow cap,
or is it his head?

And I always think I can get ahead
but when the days are packed
like so many cards into an overfull
deck, I can't do any more editing, cutting
and striking through, commenting
or giving advice. I really just want to
hear a good story, write poetry and

remind myself that

that the honeysuckle are going
to bloom in a few hours
the ones I miss every year.
This time I know why.

Puss 'N Boötes

They bloom in the cold
and the rain, in the dark
and the lightning. I put on
my mother's jean jacket with
the blue embroidery. My red kid
gloves, my clogs and I march out
to the dark field, over the trumpeting
bridge and down the gusty path
pushing me away, blinding me
eyes blearing to miss the epiphany.

Honeysuckle was the first
thing I learned to burn
on cool summer nights
snapping dead branches in the dark
kindling for bonfires
Camp meant
singing about the dear
who couldn't find water
and about Spirit then saying
goodbye to fair weather friends.

How could something
so sweet and pink,
petals like baby's eyelids
burn so bright? The flowers
are rising clouds, a spiraling
path, a universe of kisses.

Oh, to be a Honeysuckle
blossom, to always have
a twin, someone at your
back, and a crowd
of murmuring hummingbirds
so easy, so light who
think you are sustenance
for miracles.

ALICE TALKING TO FLOWERS

I hate roses, I hate roses
their thorns deadheads
the lattice cut by angry aphids

the juice of beetles, the strangling webs
In what way could this fainting beast
of a flower represent undying love?

They say every seven years
you become a completely new person
it happens one day at a time
as each fleshy cell regenerates,
over the time our little speckled egg
is slung around that solar firebird
seven times.

You'll be brand new,
it's true…

At two years old, you had
to reach up for the doorknob
to saunter down to the woods
to pick mulberries
red ones, black ones, and the ones
in between. They tasted like
nothing at all and that's
what you were wearing, who needs
clothes when the sun is warm
and candy grows on trees?

Even at two, you were ready for life
to cover you, to fill you with sweetness with
red and black and all the colors
in between…

At seven, a Kansas girl
a reader in love
with trees, books, a boy.
Jesus was your best friend.
You played checkers with Dad.

Puss 'N Boötes

Modern art something you passed
as you climbed the white steps
to a golden Buddha
with a lap big enough to
hold everyone.

This stump of knots and
broken edges, swords that could kill a man
Inside are clouds and sun
a memory of every flower back
to Adam...

At fourteen, you were a born again
teen contemplating Washington's
honest cherry blossoms,
a heart full of fireworks
and a dream to travel one
crisp apple-spin at a time.
You wrote poetry and
wove on looms to survive

Wait, leave it to the birds,
the blessed bees...

At twenty one, you still drank from the stem
of the honeysuckle in hope for nectar
for your small winged dreams.
Oh, the way it grew so profusely
the heady scent of its best evening in
May when each blossom opened times infinity—
each a double wonder heads together like two lovers
looking up to the stars.

But you painted
without color, settled for thorns because
you couldn't tell the difference.
It's the same plant, you reasoned
and your fingers bled but
you thought they were just red petals.

At twenty–eight, you lived in a cramped basement
inside a postage stamp with a new baby
with no crib for a bed but you made

apple butter from fallen fruit
and white tissue paper flowers for color.

*Why did your world keep getting
smaller when you had such big plans?
So you wrote down your dreams
and sifted them with an old window screen
to take out the big ones.
Listen, inside this death and injury
it's not what it seems. From this
misery will erupt sweet blessed
daily bread of wick green hope*

At thirty–five, you lost the farm flew in the
overnight mail with two kids and a box of paints,
They never cried while you wrote a letter
about the ocean and counted the arms of starfish,
dreaming about people underwater
because you had sunk so deep.

*When all its gruesome branches
cut down to the stub, they simply regrow
in full. First a tight fist
and then when the sun returns
an unexpected bloom.*

In just a few weeks, you will be forty–two
and have written one-third as many poems as
Emily Dickinson by wrestling with soft
scratchings and bleeding hearts pin-pricked
for words to pick locks on doors.

*Twice as old as that honeyed day,
you still miss those yellow blossoms
fallen to the cold ground, don't you.
You wish you were a honeysuckle?*

Well want about the
bud then, it's just a message
a message that somewhere
inside this death and injury
it's not what it seems.

You're an Alice,
full of red and black and all the
colors in between. Young and old,
always late. You miss moments.
You taste nothing.
Look down. See. You are
almost tripping over those branches jutted
out over your path.

Oh, it's only a wild rose— it's nothing to look at,
full of thorns, green tears for leaves
and scornful eyes of yellow pollen.

But the smell— like a dozen full roses
are in bloom even though
only five stunted petals plucked
up enough courage to show. Each petal
is a tear if you know the story.
Maybe you should be a rose instead.
The aroma. And you know what people will say when you walk by
"There is something, Now, there goes something."

It's hard to choose a side.
So I'll take both.
I'll wear my thorns as a crown. Thank you. I've
earned them, but I'll wave soft branches too.
I choose both blossoms and
sweetness, grafted, both May and June.
And with the petals I will
make a new coat, and the
honey will be ink for new words.

And this new you
this new new new new you
may she be the best one yet.

VISITED BY AN ANGEL

Once I was visited by an angel in a dream,
not like Abraham's angels. He didn't sit
down for dinner.
No, this was one tiresome
schoolmaster of an angel.
I think he wore armor.
I couldn't see him well in the dark.

All night he taught me one word
saying it over and over.

Excelsior, he'd say
Excalibur?, I'd ask
Excelsior, he'd correct me
Excelsior, I'd say–like it was
hard to form in my mouth
so foreign– so hard
to remember.

This went on for
hour upon hour
with my memory
never getting better.

In the morning, it was so
hard to remember the
word. It took me hours.

Looking back, I see now
why I couldn't hear him.
Each time he spoke
he showed me a heavy
sword. The sound of metal
upon metal so striking, its ring
covering his words.

Not long after that time,
I had another dream,
two angels this time.
I was building a house out of

honeycomb paper, empty
pretty, white as anything–
they came to carry the house away
maybe for my lost girl, I hoped.

Even though I looked it up,
excelsior became the word
I could never remember
something that meant
little pieces floating up–
bubbles, sawdust, ashes.
Nothing to do with me.
Angels–even in dreams are
myth at best I decided.

Seven years later, it's
as clear as cold water. I'm the
house and the house is me.
Looking back, I see now
why I didn't get it.
I was the empty honeycomb
dry as a paper wasps' nest,
as white as ashes. No life, no
honeyed sweetness.
Nothing could've ever lived there.

Angels called me to leave
an emptiness no one should
try to live inside of.
They sent words and weapons
and when I still sat dumbly
in a cage, they simply carried me.

They carried me away here to you,
in the promised land
I forget what it was like,
I forget what I was rescued from.

You know, I don't always see the sword in
my hand, but when I lift it up
I can still hear it ring.

EMBRACE KC— a poem with quotes by Lonnie Powell

In the dark gallery one hundred tables of
artists decked out in in dark tendrilling florals…

**But my mind was made up
by the time I was ten years old**

Lonnie Powell lifetime virtuoso achievement
award at the 17th Annnual ArtsKC Luncheon
navy as the ocean bow tie
his smile as bright as the beats
on the electronic music by Stacy Bush.

*…but I'm a girl again, growin' up in KC
Learnin' by motion and equal opposite emotion
We went places–took the bus
historic homes tours–careful of the floors
poetry readings standing room only
at the Johnson County Library.
Friends of the Zoo–I learned what a tiger
was when I looked him in the eye.*

**You better learn a trade or something.
Something people can use.**

*Abe Lincoln, I'd been to his boyhood
home, to the Ford's Theater, to his townhome,
his library, his tombstone. Metro stop, trolley, train
one drive through Mark Twain's Cave.
What I read at the library I could
call my Aunt Dorothy in Kansas
Find the Lookingglass at Grandma Alice's
house. Pour pennies into bubbling fountains.*

*In parks or churches, everywhere, anywhere
I could find a sacred hush in a brush stoke
or the face of a lion at the Nelson-Atkins Museum of Art
Every Saturday at the museum for art class,
I wore leather moccasins
through the Japanese rooms my feet making a soft*

swish over the hardwood floors.

I did what I thought I should be doing
to promote my art and to promote the art of my favorite city.

Follies and fountains
The story my family told me was *'human storytelling'*
through work and art and artwork.

'Art is not propaganda. It is a form of truth'
President Kennedy remarked.

'Workers build this ledge we stand on now, this precipice
where we have the opportunity to
reflect back the stories–high story of who we are.'

Do you see any…artists around here.
I don't see any anywhere not even in books.

"Artists aren't separate," says Nicole Emanuel
"They are Embedded. These ephemeral arts…"
she says aren't really so ephemeral, we've
always been here. *"Innovation and love"* she says
"A painter, a fire eater, and a ceramist
walk into a post office…"
and the whole room laughs
because we know the story.

Thank you to my mother for keeping me supplied with crayons
and watercolor and pencils, and lots of paper
to keep me from writing on her walls.

Some whisper—those that want to cut the arts
may be somewhere in the room.
"We are you. She tells him. We aren't separate
and we deserve to be supported and made part of the
equation."

The more he talked, the more stubborn I became,
and that's why I'm standing here

At my grandmother's house, I head to the old guest room
papered in flowers like the art by Hyeyoung Shin

I pull out a tub of paper. She saves all the junk
mail so I can make art on the back.
Next to it, a box of puzzles I like
to do sometimes. My favorite is Humpty Dumpty because
it's the hardest to put back together.

I never wanted to really be anything.
Except a teacher and an artist.

"Embedded. Ephemeral arts," says Nicole
that we've had since ancient time. But
our innovation she means– is love. *I remember*
my dad on the Starlight Theater stage
wearing a top hat, pink–cheeked
red lips, so happy and my mom
there with him singing with a feather
in her hat– just extras–I fell asleep
in my chair under the trees
and never saw the end of the show.

To my son and daughter. To my granddaughter.

"We are you.
We are allies.
We are storytellers," she adds.

I'm four years old at the Folly Theater on stage
in fishnet tights ready for my first performance
as a mermaid. My ballet shoes the size of
my father's hands. Polly at the Folly
he often said, and I would remember
dancing wearing green
tulle and sequins.

Green is for nonprofits
supporting artists who dance.
And here at the ArtsKC luncheon
I think Kansas City is my Emerald City.
Sure, we are divided but artists,
artists cross every line. Sure,
I've painted over my loses, and while
doing that, I've gained a city–size love.
I introduce my friends from each county

the curator in Wyandotte
with the curator in Johnson County.
The poets in Jackson County
with the artists in Clay.

Sure, the Star might go bankrupt but
we are all stars here and we built
this place on telling stories—we punch
out light spots in the dark matter
and nothing can quiet us. We tell stories
slant and tall—all of them are larger than life.

I always say if you meet someone from Kansas
or KC they will tell you their whole life story and
then they are your friend for life.
People say the tall tale was invented
here at the first general store in Westport by
old man Bridger. I can't help but think that what's in store
here for us after we've passed the bread and scraped the butter
we need to listen to artists.

Sure, we can rename the roads
and bridges but we have to rename our hearts
and artists are the bridge to every
part of this small Cowtown with
an Opera House.

——few people have ever seen the inside of my studio space.

The music they are playing
on stage sounds like me in the painting studio on
a normal day. First, I dance like I'm going to
GLOW. I stomp. I sing. I even whistle.
Then I begin to paint. If you wrote a
piece for a string quartet based on
what it's like to make art, I think
it would sound just like this
gentle and sweet until there's a frenzied
cacophony of color the silence after a dull roar of an
artist closing up the studio for the
night and heading home to her
kids, her dog and her mom who tells her.
Don't give up. Go to the studio.

Catch up. Paint again tomorrow.

I want to treat myself like an instrument.
If you saw this man here playing the violin,
if you saw him on the side of the road
just walking. And he didn't have his violin with him
would you know that he was a musician?
If you saw a man with dreads buying
a drink at the gas station and he wasn't
wearing his football jersey would you know
he was a KC savior? All I want to know is
why can't we know that art is our instrument

that we are all playing a song together
and some of us have strings, and some
have metal but we all play the same song?
Why can't we treat each other as instruments

playing the sound of making.
heartbeats stomping… we are making art here.
We are making art.

Thanks to my wife.
My siblings. My five brothers. I love all of you
and wouldn't change anything about you, even if I could.

"We probably agree that these are dark and stupid times,"
quotes the chairman with a paisley purple silk handkerchief
in his breast pocket, but art shouldn't be about that all the time
it can depict and it can celebrate being human.

Steinbeck says, 'The artist must believe that what he is doing
is the most important thing in the world.'

'It finds a way to depict and illuminate. Art is to recognize and
illuminate the possibilities for being human in our world,' writes
David Foster Wallace.

And to do that sometimes we have
to be deaf while making music,
blind while making art, lame while dancing, broken
while falling. Art like an egg that gets put back
together like an elephant who can fly

Art should be surprising
like jazz on a flute
like kids who are allowed to dance
like storytellers who are given a mic

It was a rainy morning five years
ago when I ran through a grey
downpour to ArtsKC.

I've opened an art gallery.

Come in, they answered.

Come in.

Easter 2020 Stay at Home

It's Easter today so I sleep in
I make soup for brunch, egg drop
for me and tomato for mom.

No one is here today and no one
is coming. Saturday the doorbell rang
a box of cookies sat there, with popcorn
and malt balls the size and color of pearls.

So I eat chocolate and think about how
I try to make my life a pearl
that's what poems are, everyone knows. Just
something we've savored, gone over
something uncomfortable we roll around
in our mouths

Faith is a pearl too always hard
putting me on edge until I accept
it's painful, impossible. Someday
I will open my mouth pull out the pearl and say

ah, here is the gate all along.

On the TV is Andrea Botticelli
the Opera singer from Il Duomo
the beautiful Italian cathedral .
he closes his eyes and looks like so many
ancient carved angels– a child's joy, a man's sorrow.

The camera shows Italy empty and so
is London, Paris and New York.
No one is out. Everyone is
staying home. The Pope cancelled
Easter and, Lord, that is saying
something.

But Il Duomo is special
my mother sang there
once with her high school choir
and the sweet notes hold in the air

for so long, she could see her life
ahead of her in that note

becoming a teacher, marrying my father.

Il Duomo only happened
because she went on a trip
with her choir director
David, a Vietnam vet who had wanted to
travel Europe but was sent to the
Jungle. I like to think that
he said, *If I ever get out of here alive*
I will go back to my hometown
and make it a pearl.

If it weren't for David, my mother
would have never met my father
on that trip in Europe when they ate
strawberry ice cream in Germany and
they called each other funny German names
for the rest of their lives.

If not for that ice cream, I wouldn't exist.
And if it wasn't for David, and the music that held
out so long in Il Duomo, the notes ringing
for what seemed like an eternity in the air—
My mother would not have taught music
then she would not have taught me to be
an artist.

And If I hadn't been an artist,
I wouldn't have taken poetry
if I hadn't taken poetry
I would not be awake or alive or even me.

So while Andrea is singing, I think that I am alive because
of a cathedral and a man who gave
high schoolers hope by giving them music
and the world in that order.

I'd like to think that we are all like David now.
Each of us is making a vow. *If I get out of here*
*alive then I will…*and we each have

a different wish, a different vow, a different
faith.

My wishes are selfish. To live on a farm and
grow a small patch of vegetables and berries.
To paint. To love. To take walks. And while I
think of planting seeds, I make my great grandmother's
dill pickles— while I make her recipe, I think of my
grandmothers and grandfathers who
gave me their pearls and their stories
and their arts. I think of my parents who
loved each other and I think of my children
who will be home at six o'clock—

I will have Easter baskets for them
with homemade chocolate hearts
melted from tiny kisses
filling their baskets with words and seeds.

And while the outside is dark
and the wind blows more fiercely and more
cold than I've ever heard in April. I will hide
100 eggs all over this blessed house
and inside those eggs are notes that say,

He is Risen. He is Alive.

I want those
kids to know where their treasure lies, for them
to have moments where a note rings out and
tells them the world may not be okay
and there may be emptiness or death
but there is a Savior who lives.

I want them to know that if we hold out
singing that note of faith, singing grace
over everything, over every empty space
we can find our way home again to each other
and to a place where pearls and gold
are just ordinary pebbles cast aside on every street.

A place where we are the treasure. We are the treasure.

YOU KNOW YOU ARE BEAUTIFUL (MAKALI'I)

One day you'll have to choose
like me to carry your heavy load
of unsaid words until you
drown in them—or
ink them into a tattoo
and limp back to shore.

You know what I decided
because here is my ink—

Let no one tell you who you are,
and what your destiny is to be.

God is love—and so love exists.

Open your mouth and tell the world
who and what you have escaped.
Taste what is good. Tell your story—

the ink running down your arm,
down to your fingertips—
that is what will guide your heart, and
your hands. Your imprint. Your
testimony is what tested you— not
what bested you.

The question is not who you are,
but what have you overcome?

Open your eyes and cry out all your salt—
for we are all going to need it to flavor our
words.

Your truth is a wall, it will be your stones,
your towers,
your flags flying.

Open your eyes. You were never
alone. God sent the wind
that carried you here.

DOE CASSEOPEIA

It's
said
that
a doe
has
smaller
horns
because
she needs
to conserve
that calcium
to bring about
new life– she's
too busy
making

life
her
wea–
pons
are
small
but her
heart
big and
who can
stand against
a mother she
will go to the
ends of the earth

walk many miles from camp to
camp she will eat nothing– and what lies she will tell. The moon
waxes outside the movie theater. Couples stroll to their cars.
A pair of barn swallows chirp and swoop for moths caught
by the buttery light.
Red   roses flash in the headlights   of
of turning cars next to David's Bridal, now dark,
there is a side lot being dug in front of an empty
field. There under the street light, a small doe—
still behind the tall grass. Her white tail
a comma, her ears glow pink. She's
made it through winter, escaped
every hunter. We stare at
each other for a long time.
She knows
the stars smell like summer.
we wonder
what each will
do next.

POLLY ALICE MCCANN poet, artist, dreamer began writing poetry after a cold winter night in the desert with only a book for her pillow. She studied poetry under Julia Kasdorf and Christine Perrin at Messiah College where she received her BA in Studio Art. After her MFA in Writing from Hamline University in St. Paul, her poetry was published internationally in journals like *365 Days*, *Naugatuck River,* and *arc24* in Tel Aviv and elsewhere. Polly's art has been published in US newspapers and magazines most recently in Rattle magazine. An adjunct writing professor and creative consultant at pollymccann.com, she is also the founder and manager of FLYING KETCHUP PRESS. She credits much of her creative work due to her research on dreams and the subconscious writing process which won her the 2014 Ernest Hartmann award from Berkeley, CA. She loves to grow basil, teach, paint, and explore unexpected surprises with her kids and their short-eared hound dog.

Poetry Prompts with Polly

Lyrical Dickinson Prompt
Round 1: Read two Emily Dickinson Poems and notice the beginning and end sounds of words.
Next. Write as many emotions into one free write poem as possible or a single deep emotion—without stopping for six minutes—
Exception: You have to write about something very, very small; insignificant.
Plus choose one unusual emotional verb (swoon, harp etc.)
and try and incorporate into the poem.

Round 2. Reread the Emily Dickinson Poem. Revise your free write poem by being intentional about alliterations and assonance and consonance as possible. Work in as many intentional sounds as you feel comfortable. Option: Rewrite the poem from that small object or animal to yourself.

Polly's Dreamscape Poetry Prompt
Round 1: Read one of Polly's poems from this book. Or Read Jane Kenyon's poem, Potato. Next, find a memory or dream to write about for six minutes. **Exception:** Make sure to choose either an object, person, or place from that specific dream or memory. Cluster your verbs around that idea.

Round 2: Look for your deepest emotion to crack open the magical moment of the poem. How? Look for a word or image that emerges, one you don't normally use in conversation. Then crack it open. Try Changing the laws of physics, or time. Do what you need to do to re-enter and change the poem to something unexpected. Try "dream entry:" Bring the dead back to life; change impossible things; time travel; do-over; or walk back into the emotion of the moment and rewrite something not quite possible. Change the equation. Try it. It feels great!

LOOK OUT FOR MORE BOOKS BY
Polly Alice McCann

Kinlight: Homegrown Poems, 2017
Tea with Alice: Heirloom Poems, 2019

COMING SOON...
Tomie Q. Barbeque 2020
Pray like a Woman 2020
How to Live Your Dreams 2021
Creative Callings 2022

FLYING KETCHUP PRESS to discover and develop new voices in poetry, drama, fiction and non–fiction with a special emphasis in new short stories. We are a publisher made by and for creatives with the spirit of the Heartland. Our dream is to salvage lost treasure troves of written and illustrated work– to create worlds of wonder and delight; to share stories. Maybe yours. Find us at www.flyingketchuppress.com.

www.ingramcontent.com/pod-product-compliance
Lightning Source LLC
Chambersburg PA
CBHW032046040426
42449CB00007B/1006